No doubt you've been bombarded with "expert" advice from your parents, professors, and countless advisors. It's time you got advice you can really use— from fellow students who've been where you're headed.

All **Students Helping Students™** guides are written and edited by top students and recent grads from colleges and universities across the U.S. You'll find no preachy or condescending advice here—just stuff to help you succeed in tackling your academic, social, and professional challenges.

Check out these other **Students Helping Students™** titles at your local or college bookstore, and online at Amazon.com, BN.com, Borders.com, and other book retailers!

Each one is packed with practical and useful advice from people who really know what they're talking about—**fellow students who've been where you're headed!**

GETTING THE MOST
FROM STUDY ABROAD

Don't sign up for a study abroad program without checking out this guide filled with tips on figuring out where and when to go, how to deal with culture shock and host family dynamics, how to choose the best classes and find local treasures, and most of all, how to truly immerse yourself in your new culture. Study abroad can be the best time of your life—pick up this guide to help you make sure that it is. *($6.95)*

SCORING A
GREAT INTERNSHIP

Finding and getting a killer internship during college has no downside— you'll learn a ton, spice up your resume, meet new people, and hopefully get a few steps closer to knowing what you'd like to do with your life after college. This guide is packed with tips on how to find the best internships, get yourself noticed and accepted, and how to learn the most once you're there. *($6.95)*

TACKLING YOUR FIRST
COLLEGE PAPER

Whether you wrote dozens of papers in high school or escaped without writing more than a few, acing your first few college papers will be a new and challenging experience. This guide will help you get ready, get organized, choose an interesting topic and a strong thesis, write a clear and error-free paper, and keep your sanity while you do it. *($6.95)*

To learn more about **Students Helping Students™** guides, read samples, share your own experiences with other students, suggest a topic or ask questions, visit us at **www.studentshelpingstudents.com**!

Students Helping Students™

FISHING FOR
A MAJOR

First Edition

NATAVI GUIDES

New York

Fishing for a Major.
First Edition.

Published by **NATAVI GUIDES**. For information on bulk purchases or custom promotional guides, please contact the publisher via email at sales@nataviguides.com or 1.866.425.4218. You can learn more about our promotional guides program on our website, www.nataviguides.com.

Printed in the U.S.A.

ISBN 0-9719392-4-1

Library of Congress Cataloging-in-Publication Data

Fishing for a major.-- 1st ed.
     p. cm. -- (Students helping students)
  ISBN 0-9719392-4-1 (pbk. : alk. paper)
  1. College majors--United States--Handbooks, manuals, etc. 2. Vocational guidance--United States--Handbooks, manuals, etc. 3. College student orientation--United States--Handbooks, manuals, etc. I. Natavi Guides (Firm) II. Series.
  LB2361.5 .F52 2002
  378.1'99--dc21

                                    2002011619

Students Helping Students™
"same pager"

Before you dive into reading this guide, we'd like to share with you a bit of the philosophy on which it's based. We figure that you'll find it more useful if we're on the same page as you begin.

We think that you're pretty smart and savvy and don't like people talking down to you.

We know that you have lots to do and are interested in reading only the most relevant information.

We believe that you appreciate the value of advice given by someone who has been where you're going.

And one more thing: Don't just read this guide. <u>USE IT</u> to help you get where you're going. Write in it and on it, fold pages you find useful and refer to them later, carry it in your bag for good luck. Do whatever it is that will help you tackle the tasks before you!

the primary author

Julio Machado is studying history and literature at Harvard University. He has written other guides for college students, including several literature study guides and a handbook for writing the perfect application essay. As of this guide's publication date, he's still working on his first great novel, which should be completed within the next fifty to sixty years.

the contributors

Students from Boston University, Brown University, Carleton College, Cornell University, Florida International University, Georgia Tech, Harvard University, Stanford University, the University of Colorado – Boulder, the University of Florida, the University of Massachusetts – Amherst, the University of Rhode Island, Wellesley College, Wesleyan University, and Yale University contributed to this guide.

author's note

In one of my high school English classes, we were once given a worksheet entitled "Can you follow directions?" The first line on the worksheet said, "Read everything on this page before commencing," and there followed a series of forty commands for us to follow. Write your name on the top right corner, draw a triangle, stand up and say, "I've reached line twenty!" etc. The fortieth command read, "Only do commands one and forty."

After half an hour, we dejectedly submitted our worksheets to the teacher. Those of us who had taken the first line seriously had spent only a few minutes on the worksheet; the rest of us had scribbled all over the page and made fools of ourselves shouting out random things. Needless to say, nearly everyone in the class was in the second group.

So what happened? Why did everyone follow the forty commands so scrupulously and ignore the very first? The answer to this question is an important factor in determining whether or not you'll find anything useful in this guide: As human beings, we often ignore things that we believe we already understand.

We've tried to collect a lot of useful advice in this guide, and some of it will undoubtedly sound familiar to you. Figuring out what you should major in isn't rocket science, and we can't claim to give you a secret tip no one else has thought of before. But if you pay some attention to the advice your fellow students have shared in this guide, you might think of a thing or two that helps you find a major that genuinely interests you and makes your college experience a great one.

contents

what it is

Choosing a field of study, or a major, is in many ways a process of self-discovery. It's the search for what you're truly interested in, for what you feel you can happily study for the four years you spend in college. As you begin to consider your academic career, ask yourself, "What do I *really* love to do?" If the answer is simple and immediate, and there exists an appropriate academic field, then your path is clear. Don't worry too much whether someone will actually pay you money to do what you love or if your major will make your parents proud. If you're happy and learning about something you genuinely find interesting, you'll find a way to make it work.

If you don't know what you love, or if what you love can't possibly translate into academic study, then there are steps you can take to figure out your ambitions and interests. Choosing a major can be a long and sometimes frustrating journey into the academic world. There will be days when you simply refuse to think about your future as it rushes toward you like a locomotive. You'll want to tear your student handbook to pieces as you wonder again and again, "*Why* do I have to choose a major?" Even if you read every word in this guide, you may still run into the same issues.

Like many other big decisions, choosing a field of study will be as fruitful a process as you're willing to make it. If you're honest with yourself—if you finally admit that you hate chemistry and would much rather spend your time reading about American history, for example—then your chances of having a great college experience will be pretty high. If you shy away from facing reality, or just simply don't put too much thought into finding a major that makes you happy, you'll run the risk of making yourself miserable. We vote for the former.

what it's not

Choosing a major is not a curse thrown upon you by evil academic forces. The process can be frustrating—too little advising, too much pressure to choose right away, etc. But you should keep in mind that choosing a major is an important part of your college experience and one that's worth carefully thinking about. The world is much too vast to tackle all at once. You have to stake your claim on a little piece of it and build a home.

Choosing a major is not irrelevant or unimportant. Your field of study will speak to you constantly—through advisors, professors, course requirements, and fellow students. Whatever choices you make after college, your chosen major will continue to matter through the years. It will affect you, enrich your mind, expand your options, and for some, define the course of your life. Make an effort to find the right major, and you might get more out of college than you ever expected.

Your major is not something that will necessarily monumentally and irreversibly affect the rest of your life. There are so many great things to learn about that you could spend your college years studying something very interesting without it actually relating in any way to your future career. On the flip side, if you absolutely despise what you study in college, it doesn't mean that you'll be miserably stuck with it for the rest of your life.

getting acquainted
with yourself

There are many ways to choose a major—random selection, choosing the first thing that comes to mind, pin-the-tail-on-the-major, etc. If your goal is to make your college years as productive and rewarding as possible, you should seriously consider a more organized and thoughtful approach. You've probably heard it a million times: You need to get to know yourself. Take a minute this time and read the words carefully: K-n-o-w Y-o-u-r-s-e-l-f. The greatest service you can do yourself and your potential major is to seek out your interests and embrace them.

"But," you might say, "what if I can't figure out what I want to do for the rest of my life?" Truth is, you don't have to know and you probably shouldn't. College is the ideal place to explore your interests and develop new ones. You'll probably feel an immense pressure to choose a career path and stick to it, but you have to be strong and resist it for at least a short while. Even if you're pretty sure that you know where you're headed, it can't hurt to take a look around.

C'mon, what do you have to lose?

ASSESS YOUR STRENGTHS AND WEAKNESSES
▼

THINK ABOUT YOUR GOALS
▼

RESEARCH MOST LIKELY MAJORS
▼

VENTURE INTO UNFAMILIAR DISCIPLINES

ASSESS YOUR STRENGTHS AND WEAKNESSES

"Don't do what you think will get you a lot of money or what other people tell you to do, but do what you really enjoy."

Visual and Environmental Studies major, Harvard University '03

This may seem like a rather obvious step, but far too many of us enter college with a particular career in mind and we choose our majors accordingly. Your parents will probably be pretty happy if you choose the security and financial rewards of a pre-med or business track, but you might be dooming yourself to four years of misery—or many more. Open your mind to every possibility before narrowing down your choices.

Begin by asking yourself: What am I really good at? Were you a history whiz in high school, or did you sometimes find yourself explaining math homework to other students? Often being good at something means that you're interested in and passionate about it. Interest and passion are exactly what you're after in a major.

If you're feeling very organized, make a list of your skills and strengths, and don't leave anything out because it seems irrelevant—foot massages, juggling, Trivial Pursuit, or whatever you naturally do well. This list will serve as a general framework as you begin to major hunt.

Next, think about the things you love to do—reading, jogging, traveling, etc.—and try to include some academic things as well. If you're having a hard time thinking of real interests, then you may need to take some time and get to know yourself. Think about your high school and junior high experiences. When did you feel most comfortable or most excited about what you were doing? Was there ever a moment when you thought, "I think I'd enjoy doing this for the rest of my life." Grab those moments and remember them as you begin to consider potential fields of study.

Finally, keep in mind that there may be fields you've never encountered or considered that could make you infinitely happy. If you're the kind of person who enjoys being challenged, then your college years will allow you to explore vast tracts of uncharted territory, and you may discover a few surprises along the way. Leave a few blank spaces at the end of every list you make for the strengths and interests that you never knew you had.

THINK ABOUT YOUR GOALS

"I've always thought I'd be the starving artist type, but then I ran into some money problems sophomore year and I had to eat ramen noodles for three weeks. I still want to be an artist, but I want to be well fed."

**Music Theory major,
Cornell University '02**

So, where do you want your life to go? If this question makes your head spin in confusion, then you're just about where most of us are as we begin our college experience. It's okay not to know yet, no matter what anyone tells you.

In junior high and high school, we don't usually get to know what the world is really like. College is a great place to begin to do this. Try not to be too intimidated by the experience of figuring out what you like to do in life so much so that you don't try and think about it.

Of course, you probably *do* have some goals. You might even have it all figured out—or you might think you do. Before you start choosing classes, ask yourself, "What do I want to be doing in ten years?" Depending on how narrow or broad your answer is ("I want to be eating three meals a day" is not a useful place to start), you'll find that every goal acts as a guide for your course selections. If you think you might want to be a doctor, you'll need to take some introductory biology and chemistry courses. If you think you want to go into business, you should think about taking an econ class to begin to learn about it.

You should always keep in mind, however, that your goals can and will change. The more you learn, the more sophisticated and potentially rewarding your career decisions will be. Keep your options open at all times. Take a wide variety of courses and pursue every possible interest. Let the four years you spend in college affect your career—and life—aspirations: The world will be very different by the time you graduate, and you'll have to be prepared to deal with this new reality.

author's corner
▼
When I first started college, I was thinking about studying computer science as a way to earn a big salary and support my writing career. I thought I might develop some brilliant new method for generating artificial intelligence as I worked on a groundbreaking novel in my plentiful leisure time. I later realized that four years was a long time to

study something I only half-liked, and I began looking for a better option.

▲

RESEARCH MOST LIKELY MAJORS

"I took a few classes, but mostly I looked at all the concentrations and asked, which one of these interests me the most, and that's where I started researching. I also looked at the requirements for some of them, which courses I had to take and how many."

Government and Philosophy major, Harvard University '03

Based on your interests and goals, it should be fairly easy to construct a list of five to seven fields that appeal to you. Let's call these your "probable" majors. Each of these majors is a potential home for you, but you have to devote some time to exploring it. You might find that what looks to be appealing on the outside is not as great as it seems when you really dive into it.

Keep in mind that college majors tend to be very broad and comprehensive. Just because you really love a certain book doesn't mean that you should become an English major, and just because you loved your summer trip to Chile shouldn't necessarily lead you to study Latin American history. Think realistically about your interests and corresponding fields of study so you won't be shocked when you discover that what you thought was a perfect match really isn't. And when you do find a probable major, write it down.

YOUR LIST OF PROBABLE MAJORS

Give it a shot—no matter how much you might hate making lists. Don't be afraid to include less-than-certain possibilities. The key here is "probable."

1. _____

2. _____

3. _____

4. _____

5. _____

6. _____

7. _____

VENTURE INTO UNFAMILIAR DISCIPLINES

"If I had to choose now, I probably would have studied Economics. I hated Economics at the time I was choosing my major, but I didn't really know a whole lot about it."

**Computer Science major,
Harvard University '03**

As you look through your list of probable majors, keep in mind that there are many, many fields that you've never really had time to explore. Where else are you going to get that chance if not in college? You may think you understand every field out there (that is, you've got the "gist"), but you won't know unless you make the effort to venture into unfamiliar territory and explore all of your options. At worst, you'll spend a few credits; at best, you'll discover a potentially life-altering new passion.

Pay particular attention to fields that you didn't have the chance to explore in high school. Colleges tend to offer much broader variety than most high schools, and you may have never had the opportunity to study things like Sanskrit or neurobiology until now.

Use your school's course catalogue as your first research tool. Browse through the listings and force your eyes to pause on pages you'd never thought to consider. Are you an artist at heart? Peruse the computer science or economics section for more than ten seconds, if you can take it. Are you a hardcore statistics buff? Check out history or philosophy courses. You might surprise yourself.

As you explore new fields of study, keep track of what appeals to you. A newly found interest might not turn into a major, but you might choose it as a minor, or it might turn into a special project within your major. In the chapters that follow, we'll discuss a process through which you can research, understand, and nail down your ideal major. As you go through it, be sure to keep with you your list of "never-thought-I'd-like-this-but-I-might majors." If your college experience is at all typical, you'll probably end up choosing something you never expected.

author's corner
▾

Freshman year I was like a chipmunk on speed. I woke up every morning with the kind of energy the gods must have, and it never seemed to run out. If you've just started college, you might still be feeling this kind of excitement. My advice to you is to take advantage of it while it lasts: Plan ahead, make schedules, and set goals. In a few months, when the high has begun to wear off, you'll still have these plans to follow and you'll be incredibly thankful.
▲

NEW FIELDS TO CONSIDER

Don't know much about Anthropology but find the name interesting? Always wondered if you should pursue your painting more seriously? Add it to your list of academic fields that you want to explore.

1. _____

2. _____

3. _____

4. _____

5. _____

6. _____

7. _____

thinking about your career

As you begin to think about your major, more likely than not thoughts and questions about what you'll do with your life after college will creep into your mind. Will a degree in Music Theory help you feed your children and pay the utility bills? Do you need to major in economics to become an entrepreneur? Can you major in philosophy and still go on to medical school and become a doctor?

It's a good idea to give your potential career some thought, but what we don't recommend is that you obsess about and choose a major that you think will lead to it. You should choose a major that lets you study things that you really enjoy. If you enjoy them, there is at least a chance that you will want to have a post-college job that has something to do with them.

Also keep in mind that what you do outside of class—during an internship or as an extracurricular activity—can have as much, if not more, impact on your future career as your major. Just because you major in English doesn't mean that you'll like journalism; but if you love writing for your school paper, it might mean that a journalist is deep within you.

KNOW THAT MAJOR DOESN'T MEAN CAREER

▼

TALK TO RECENT GRADS

▼

VISIT THE CAREER SERVICES OFFICE

▼

KNOW YOUR REQUIREMENTS

▼

DON'T IGNORE EXTRACURRICULARS

KNOW THAT MAJOR DOESN'T MEAN CAREER

"Don't think that because you want to go into business that you have to study business. If you want to be an artist, you don't necessarily have to study art. When I look at a resume, I don't look for a particular degree. I ask myself, what can this person bring to the job that no one else can? I can teach you to use business software; I can't duplicate the kind of growth you get from four years of college."

Branch Manager, Ford Motors, Inc.,
Music major,
Alabama State University '71

Unless you go to a vocational college—in which case you're clearly there to learn specific skills for a certain career—you shouldn't think of your major as a way to prepare for a certain job after you graduate. Or even as a way to find out what type of job you'd like to have. Just because you take and love every psychology class offered in the curriculum doesn't mean that you'll love being a psychologist. And not doing well in your econ class doesn't mean that your dream to become an entrepreneur is any less real. (In fact, many people working in business today don't have business or economics degrees. Music and history majors often end up as branch managers or entrepreneurs, and they thrive in their positions.)

Try not to worry about knowing what you want to do after college, at least for a few years. You'll have all the time in the world—including the last few years of college—to think about and figure out what your post-college job might be.

But you won't have another opportunity like this to really explore different academic fields, learn the different skills that they offer, and train your mind to think about things as different as art history and statistics. An English class won't completely prepare you for a career in publishing, but it will teach you how to write well, and that's a skill that you definitely want to acquire.

If you choose a major that truly interests you and pushes you to learn, you'll gain a huge set of skills that you can then use in any career. It sounds so idealistic, but it's true. Employers don't expect you to start your first job knowing exactly how to do it—on-the-job training is a core learning component that almost all careers offer. But employers do expect you to be a well-rounded person, have solid writing and communication skills, and the ability and training to learn new things and excel at them.

TALK TO RECENT GRADS

"I've wanted to be a doctor since I was four, so when I got to college, I was pretty much set on majoring in Biology or Organic Chemistry or something like that. After talking to a few medical school students, though, I discovered that the best majors are the unexpected ones. That's how I ended up in the Psychology department."

**Psychology major,
UMass - Amherst '02**

Your potential future career and your college major may not and don't need to have much in common. But if you do have some career ideas in mind and you'd like to know what kinds of classes and fields you might find useful, consider seeking out some recent grads and talking to them. Do you need to study art history to manage an art gallery? Does a math major mean that you'll have a hard time getting a job in the music industry? Recent grads are still fresh on their college experience and have tasted a bit of the real career world—they can offer some useful ideas and are pretty easy to find.

You might know some recent grads in your family, among your friends, or people you've worked with. Give them a call, see how they are, and tell them about your quest for a major. If there's one thing we've learned in writing this guide it's that people love to talk about themselves. Don't worry about imposing on their time—who doesn't like to be asked for their sage advice?

If you don't personally know any recent grads, you should pay a visit to your school's career center. You'll probably find an alumni database that you can search by location, career, year of graduation, and even major. Use it to find a few recent grads who're doing what you might like to be doing in a few years. Send them an email to introduce yourself and explain why you've taken an interest in their particular situation. But make it very clear that what you're looking for is advice and not a job.

Many alumni are overloaded with requests for jobs or internships that are disguised as requests for advice, and most don't like any of these sneaky maneuvers. Avoid bad first impressions by clearly stating that you're in the process of searching for a major and would like some advice. Pay some compliments—it will get you everywhere. For example: "I think your job as a (fill in the blank) sounds wonderful and I'd like to find out how your college experience helped you get to this point."

If you get a positive response, arrange to talk by phone, if possible. Jot down some *specific* questions to give the conversation some structure because phone silence can be some of the most uncomfortable in the world. Here are some examples of what you might want to ask:

- What was your major and how did you end up choosing it?

- Could you tell me about what you did after college and how you got to your current job?

- Do you think that I should major in (fill in the blank) to be able to get a job in your field?

- What are some important skills I should aim to get in order to succeed in your career?

- Do you think it really matters what I major in with respect to being able to get a job in your industry?

And make sure to thank whomever you talk to—besides being polite, you want to leave a good impression in case you do need to discuss job opportunities in the future.

VISIT THE CAREER SERVICES OFFICE

The career services office at your school is a great resource to help you sort out your ideas about what major you might choose and how it might relate to the few career choices you're contemplating. If you can, definitely spend some time with a career counselor. Although you might feel that career counselors are reserved for those actively looking for a job, they aren't. They're there to talk to all students and can be extremely helpful. Go ahead and set up an appointment and you might be surprised at the advice you receive.

Talk to a career counselor about your interests and your goals, including what you think you might want to do with your life after graduation. Try not to focus so much on a particular career at this point, but rather, on things that you would like to be doing—painting, teaching, traveling, researching, interacting with people, building skyscrapers, and so on. Career counselors probably interact with more students and alumni than most other advisors on campus, and they learn quite a bit about the paths that students take and the majors that lead them there.

If a particular college major is critical for your desired career, then visiting the career services office is not an option, but a requirement. Here you'll find detailed job descriptions, alumni databases, and a dozen other useful sources. Make sure to also check graduate school information and related requirements.

And don't miss out on taking a career aptitude test, if you can find one. While you might think you know exactly what you want to do, it never hurts to explore your options.

author's corner
▼
Don't dismiss career aptitude tests entirely. The questions on those things tend to be loaded ("Do you like to work with heavy machinery?"), so that you're always double-guessing the test. If you do your best to avoid doing this, though, you can get a pretty good reading on your skills. I

took an aptitude test in elementary school and it told me I was going to be a writer. Go figure.

▲

KNOW YOUR REQUIREMENTS

"The best candidates are well-balanced. We get so many biology and physiology majors applying here, it's refreshing to see someone who studied environmental science or computer engineering."

**Admissions Officer, UCLA School of Medicine,
Physical Sciences major,
University of California - Berkeley '82**

For those of you who hope to become doctors, lawyers, or career academics, the courses you take now will be an important part of your overall career development. You should make sure that you know if there are any specific course requirements and allow time in your four-year schedule to get them done.

If you're planning to go on to medical school, for example, you have no choice but to fulfill the required courses, like the often-dreaded organic chemistry. Your choice of major, however, offers surprising flexibility. Don't get locked into the obvious choices right away—biology, political science, etc. There are many ways to meet your pre-med or pre-law requirements, and you should seriously consider selecting an unrelated primary major and meeting those requirements on the side.

DON'T IGNORE EXTRACURRICULARS

No doubt, college is the perfect place to explore and find what you enjoy doing and learning about. But going to class and majoring in a certain subject is just one way to do that. Another great way to try out different things and see if any one of them spikes your passions is to get involved in extracurricular activities. As you think about your career, don't feel the need to have a major that fits perfectly with it.

If you're interested in working in the music industry, for instance, you might be doing yourself a far greater service by joining your school's radio station or securing an internship at a recording studio than by studying modern media. If you're thinking about being a teacher, studying early childhood psychology won't really tell you what it's like to work with kids—but volunteering as a tutor will.

> *"I always thought that I wanted to be an English teacher. But when I got the chance to get into an actual classroom as a tutor, I realized that too much of my time was spent being a policeman instead of talking about the beauty of Shakespeare's sonnets."*
>
> **English major,**
> **Wesleyan University '99**

In other words, don't put all the pressure of finding out what you like to do and what you'd like to do as a career on your major. Talking to people around you, finding out about potential careers, getting internships, becoming involved in extracurricular activities, and just learning about things that people do in the world will all help you figure out what it is that you want to do. Your major should be something that interests you and makes you excited to learn, and it's not necessarily something that you can practically integrate into your future career.

talking to your peers

One of the most important sources of information available to you is your fellow students. They can give you insights into everything from particular courses to academic departments to local movie theaters. They've been through it, and they've gathered a few bits of useful information along the way. More importantly, they tend to be brutally honest when discussing professors and programs—you'll get the kind of information that you just can't find in any booklet.

Whatever you do, make sure you talk to *someone*. Hearsay is an important part of the decision-making process—gossip, movie reviews, safety ratings—we use hearsay all the time, and our lives are much easier because of it. Some sources will be more trustworthy than others, and this is where you must make your own judgments.

To gain the most from talking to other students, try to get a sampling of opinions and advice from people with diverse levels of experience and hindsight. Here are a few groups to consider.

TALK WITH FELLOW UNDERGRADS
▼

SEEK OUT DEPARTMENT INSIDERS
▼

ASK GRAD STUDENTS

TALK WITH FELLOW UNDERGRADS

"If it hadn't been for my roommates, I wouldn't have taken some of my favorite classes. If you're lucky enough to know a few people who share your outlook, you can learn from their mistakes and profit from their discoveries."

Physical Sciences major,
University of California - Berkeley '03

The first and most obvious place to go for honest advice is your fellow classmates, particularly upperclassmen who've been through just about everything you're about to experience. They tend to be more approachable than professors or graduate students, and they're more likely to understand your particular concerns. Just remember that everyone has subjective tastes and biases, and you should take opinions and complaints with a grain of salt.

"I would say hearsay is important. You can't believe everything you hear, but you can believe most of it."

History and Literature lecturer,
Harvard University

One of the best pieces of information your fellow students can share is the quality of different classes and professors. It's tough to judge what a class might be like from its description in the course catalogue, so ask students who've taken it. What material is covered? How interesting is it?

How involved are the students in class discussion? Make sure to also get honest opinions about professors—they can make or break a class. Ask other students about their quality of teaching, how enthusiastic and accessible they are, and so on. (Be careful when you ask about specific classes, though. If your school has an honor code, it may be forbidden to ask about the *difficulty* of courses or the materials included in past examinations.)

When asking fellow students about a particular class, remember that there are many reasons for disliking a course—and not all of them are easy to admit. Some students will complain about a professor's teaching style or the irrelevance of the readings, when in fact they attended only a few of the lectures and did only a fraction of the reading. You'll find that the slacker is a perennial source of misinformation, and that it's almost impossible to get a straight answer from the ultra-competitive crowd. Aim for students with similar interests and priorities to your own— they're more likely to give you useful information.

You'll also find it useful to talk to other students about the actual process of choosing a major. Where did they get the most helpful advice? Did auditing a few classes help or confuse them? What were some of the concerns that guided their decisions? Ask around, and try not to dismiss anything just because it seems strange or different.

SEEK OUT DEPARTMENT INSIDERS

Aside from helping you choose courses, interviewing fellow students can help you get to know departments and fields from an undergraduate perspective. A great deal of material is probably available online and in course catalogues, but it's difficult to sift through it all without some guidance. Once you choose a field, you'll have an advisor and a set of recommended reading materials to help you make the transition.

But before that happens—if you want to explore your options without making a serious commitment—your best bet is to talk to upperclassmen within the particular department. So you think you might want to major in math? Ask math majors what they think about their professors, their advisors, and their requirements—you might discover that your school's math program isn't so great. Maybe history's your thing? Ask history majors what they think of their particular concentrations and whether they wish they'd chosen something different—you might discover that Latin American history professors aren't up to par with the rest of the department. Don't shy away from finding this out—better now than later.

"I wish I'd spoken to someone before taking some of the classes I took. I wasted a lot of time taking terrible courses that weren't even required."

**Economics major,
Boston University '03**

author's corner
▼
I discussed my plan to study Computer Science with a friend of mine who was about to graduate with a degree in Applied Math, and what he told me quite possibly saved my academic career. It was this: "Don't even think about doing that. Study what you like. If you hate it in college, you're going to hate it all your life."
▲

ASK GRAD STUDENTS

Another great source of information and department gossip—which is extremely valuable information—is grad students. Most graduate programs require students to undertake two years of advanced coursework toward a Master's or Ph.D. The average graduate student thus has between four and six years of experience in his or her field. This translates into a lot of individual classes and a lot of personal discovery. If you can tap into this kind of information, you'll make your own path much easier.

In many colleges, larger courses are taught or graded by graduate students who work closely with the professor and typically assist with research. These students can be an extremely valuable source of information about a particular field.

It takes a certain kind of person to pursue graduate studies—only the most dedicated or the most interested make it past college—and so you'll probably find that your T.A. *loves* to talk about his or her field. If you ask the right questions, you'll get more information than you know what to do with.

working with advisors

Maybe it's because we don't like being told what to do, or because our high school guidance counselors weren't always helpful. But it seems that we often forget just how valuable our school's advising system might be—for help with choosing a major as well as many other academic issues.

Most colleges and universities have a formal academic advising program in place. All of them have professors and career counselors, and these people can be a great source of knowledge, help, and advice, and many of them are dying to help if only you'd ask. Make these people happy. At worst, you'll learn nothing new. At best, you'll find a source of inspiration, support, and good advice about figuring out your major.

MEET WITH YOUR ACADEMIC ADVISOR
▼

TALK TO PROFESSORS
▼

GO OUTSIDE THE SYSTEM

MEET WITH YOUR ACADEMIC ADVISOR

"I was assigned an advisor right off the bat, but I didn't talk to her for months. I'm sorry I didn't go earlier, though. She was so helpful."

**Economics major,
Boston University '03**

When you begin your freshman year, you'll probably be assigned an academic advisor. Depending on your school's advising policy, this person may be a professor, a dean, or a full-time counselor. In many cases, your advisor will not belong to the academic department that you're hoping to explore. This doesn't mean, however, that you can't get useful information from him or her. Rather, you should understand the limitations of your advisor's knowledge and seek outside help when necessary.

Although your advisor might not know everything about your particular fields of interest, he or she can be quite helpful in a general sense. You can discuss your ambitions, your concerns, and anything else that might be affecting your major-selection process. If nothing else, your assigned advisor can point you to the right places to go for more detailed and specific advice, and can be a good source for logistical information—when you must declare your major, what forms need to be filled out, etc.

Another resource that too few students seem to take advantage of is departmental advising. There are usually two or three people within every department whose primary duties are to help prospective students within that major/field. These people will help you get to know the department before you join, which will give you plenty of time to avoid leaping into unfriendly waters. They can also help you sort out the mess of credit-hour requirements that will undoubtedly haunt you for the rest of your college days. Not sure if that government class counts toward your political science track? Wondering if you can substitute your AP scores for introductory science classes? Departmental advisors can give you answers to these kinds of questions, but you're going to have to ask them first.

Once you choose a major, you'll probably be assigned to an advisor from that department. While policy on this varies from school to school, you should try to make sure that your advisor's specialty is as close to your intended program as possible. As your academic years progress, the issues you face become more and more complex—where to concentrate within your major, what to write your thesis about, where to apply to graduate school—and you'll need to have an advisor who knows a great deal about very particular problems.

Whatever you do, don't settle for sub-par advising. If your advisor seems confused or uninformed, pay a few discreet visits to other advisors in the department. You might find someone who's more willing to help, or is more receptive to your way of doing things. If your school allows it, switch to this advisor as soon as possible. Above all, be honest about your needs and concerns. Let your old advisor know why you're going elsewhere and give specific reasons whenever you can. He or she may not appreciate being dumped (who would?), but you won't leave room for argument if you come prepared.

TALK TO PROFESSORS

While you're storming your school's advising system, don't neglect another valuable resource of information and advice about majors—professors. You can choose whatever major you like, but unless its core classes are taught by intriguing and knowledgeable professors who are interested in their students, you'll miss out on a great education.

You've probably heard a few seniors or recent grads say that it was a few special professors that made their college education a great investment, and we think that's a great point to keep in mind. As you shop around for a major, you have to make sure that its faculty is as great as you'd like your professors and advisors to be—the quality of your professors can make or break your college experience.

Find out what professors teach courses in the fields you're interested in and go see them. Most hold office hours and some even devote a few office hours each month to speaking with prospective majors. Since current students frequent office hours to discuss assignments and class projects, you'll be a fresh and welcome change for the professor. Talk to him or her about the particular academic field, its core courses, and the professor's own academic interests. See if the professor is excited and engaged by what he or she is talking about, and whether this is someone you'd learn a lot from as a student.

You might not find that you like every professor you meet, but if you put in some effort and go to see a few of them in your potential majors, you'll have a much better idea of which field is best for you.

GO OUTSIDE THE SYSTEM

"When I registered for classes, my 'advisor' was about ten years old. He didn't seem to know the answers to any of my questions."

**Math and Electrical Engineering major,
Florida International University '03**

Unfortunately, not every school has a well-established or experienced advising system. You may find that your school's guidance counselors are only a couple of years older than you—if that—and you can't seem to get any straight answers from them. In this kind of environment, your best bet is to try and tiptoe around the front line of advisors and attack the commanding officers.

Go to the advising office website (if it exists) and find out who the bosses are. Call these people and set up appointments—they're usually required to meet with students and are happy to do so. If there isn't a website, try to find a staff directory or an office pamphlet. Put some effort into this, it'll make a difference.

There's also a chance that even after you talk to advisors, professors, and career counselors, you still won't feel like you've gotten enough information to make an intelligent decision. Think of other resources you might use—friends in other colleges, academic deans, and even your parents. The main thing to remember is that you should take as much time as you need to find out as much information as you need in order to make a choice that has quite a bit of impact on how you spend—and enjoy—your time in college.

choosing classes

"The concept that should rule [when choosing classes] is shopping: Look around, see what you like."

**History and Literature lecturer,
Harvard University**

Ultimately, the only way to really get to know a field is to take a few courses in that department. It's not enough that you took similar classes in high school, or that you've read some related books (unless, of course, you've read *all* the books). You won't know for sure what interests you and what doesn't until you've done some real coursework, and you won't do any coursework unless you take some courses.

You won't always have the luxury of choice—your college will probably require that you take some classes that you'd never otherwise consider—but even within the tightest requirements, you'll still have a little room to maneuver. Find a few courses that truly interest you and try to fit them into your schedule.

And as you go about selecting your classes, be gutsy and venture into some unknown areas, as well as those that you think you might major in.

EXPLORE CLASSES IN LIKELY MAJORS
▼

VENTURE INTO THE UNKNOWN
▼

TAKE ADVANTAGE OF THE CORE CURRICULUM
▼

MAKE EVERY CLASS COUNT

EXPLORE CLASSES IN LIKELY MAJORS

"The first classes I looked at were business classes. I'd always wanted to study business, so that's where I started when I had to register."

**Business major,
University of Colorado - Boulder '01**

Remember that list of your probable majors? Use it as you look through your course catalogue to select a few classes. If you're a freshman or sophomore, your options will be somewhat limited by particular course requirements. Don't let this bother you too much. You can learn a lot from these intro classes, and the broader knowledge will probably come in handy later.

If you can manage it, go beyond the standard introductory courses—be courageous and take a few that are more advanced. Course material inevitably becomes more specific and demanding as you delve deeper into your field, and harder classes will give you a chance to test your ability to handle increasing levels of specificity. They'll also help you decide if this is the type of material that you want to learn about in tremendous depth over the course of a few years. You might find that computer science is too theory-intensive for your tastes or that art history relies too heavily on classification and codification to suit your style.

VENTURE INTO THE UNKNOWN

"Take the time to really read the course catalogue. Don't just look for stuff you think first-years should take."

**English and Music major,
Wellesley College '03**

Above all, take a chance. Enroll in a few classes that you might have never considered. Try a few that seem intimidatingly different from the classes to which you're usually drawn. Allow that other side of your brain to get some nourishment, and you might surprise yourself.

You have a very unique opportunity in college to explore your intellect and your passions, so take advantage of it while you can. You might absolutely despise the class you take—and blame us for making you sit through hours of torture—but you'll save yourself a lot of "what ifs" later on.

Try not to assume that just because you didn't do well in a particular discipline in high school, you can't be interested in it and ace it in college. High school classes can be pretty boring and not all teachers are inspiring. One great English prof in college can turn you onto Shakespeare in just a few weeks.

Besides, learning what you don't like is just as critical as finding out what genuinely interests you.

TAKE ADVANTAGE OF THE CORE CURRICULUM

"If I hadn't had to take a history core course, I'd be studying engineering right now. My parents are pissed, but I'm happy."

**American History major,
Stanford University '02**

In the last fifty years, many schools have adopted a "Core System" in order to give their students a well-rounded liberal education. The most common version consists of specialized introductory courses in several broad fields— literature, history, physical science, etc. Within this system, we're required to take at least a few courses in each of these fields before we graduate.

For many of us, the core curriculum might be an irritating distraction in an already difficult and confusing environment (if you feel this way, you're not alone, as a new wave of education scholars has come to question the utility of liberal arts requirements). Whatever your view on this might be, chances are that your school will have some kind of a requirement system in place.

If you're stuck with requirements, you might as well take advantage of them. If you have to fulfill a history requirement, for example, choose an area of the world that interests you. For a literature requirement, consider taking a class that covers a book or an author that you like. There's bound to be a class or two within each discipline that interests you, so find it.

A core curriculum can be an important element in your quest to find a major—it forces you to take classes in a variety of disciplines, some of which you might have never otherwise considered. If you'll pardon the cliché—you'll never know unless you try.

MAKE EVERY CLASS COUNT

If you care enough to read this guide, we probably don't need to remind you that a class is only worth as much as the effort and interest you invest in it. But we can all use a few reminders now and then, so here it goes.

Just about every student we talked to agrees on this much—you absolutely have to go to lectures. Whatever else you do, going to class will keep you in touch with the course and its particular approach to the subject. Why go to college if you're not going to make it to class? You can read books and write papers on your own time; you have to go to *college* to attend lectures.

In larger courses, lectures will let you see how your professor interprets the material and help you stay on schedule and learn of important events ahead of time (you can't trust email or course websites for this). In smaller courses, going to class will also give you the opportunity to get to know your fellow students, from whom you can probably learn as much as from the professors and books you're assigned.

Which brings us to the next bit of advice: Put some effort into getting to know your professors. Make a little time and go to office hours. Ask your professors about their research, get their thoughts on their departments, and bring them questions about assignments and course materials.

You'll find that you enjoy a course much more if you actually know the professor, and every lecture will seem more relevant and engaging. While many professors seem too busy to talk to students, they actually like and respect students who make a little extra effort.

author's corner

▼

I finally took the leap my sophomore year and went to my history professor's office hours. I composed a list of questions I wanted to ask about the books she'd assigned us. When I finally got there, I found three other students hogging her attention. They were asking her almost exactly what I'd intended to ask and I quickly left, feeling embarrassed that I'd intended to be so obvious. I came back the next week and found her alone. I sat down across from her and asked, "So... how about those Patriots?" I run into her sometimes, and she still remembers my name.

▲

If you fall behind on the reading in a certain class, don't try to catch up unless you can do it quickly. Lagging behind the class will diminish your sense of belonging—you'll grow increasingly detached from the course and its progress, making it harder for you to understand what's going on. Do as much of each week's reading as you can and then move on—even if it means getting less from individual assignments.

settling down

"Try to put your decision off as long as you can, so that you know as much as possible."

**Computer Science major,
Harvard University '03**

As soon as you start college, you're going to feel it: The pressure coming in from all directions—the pressure to choose a major and stick to it. Whatever you do, try to resist that pressure for as long as you can. Contrary to popular belief, you *do* have some time (usually at least three full semesters) in which to explore potential fields and take interesting courses. It helps to know from day one what you want to do for the rest of your life, but it's not necessary or likely. Spend your first one or two years exploring your interests and the academic fields you might like to study in depth.

There will naturally come a day when you do have to make a decision, but if you've followed even some of the advice in this guide, you'll be well prepared. Take a breath and dive into it, as you keep in mind the following points.

WEIGH YOUR OPTIONS
▼

CONSIDER A DOUBLE MAJOR
▼

THINK ABOUT DESIGNING YOUR OWN MAJOR
▼

DON'T NEGLECT MINORS AND CONCENTRATIONS
▼

MAKE UP YOUR MIND

WEIGH YOUR OPTIONS

Once you've taken a few introductory and mid-level courses, talked with a few professors and advisors, and thought long and hard about your own interests, you'll have a much better idea of where you want to go. Think about the classes you've taken so far. Which were your favorites? Was there ever a point at which you were genuinely excited by the things you were studying? If you take the time and consider your experiences, you'll probably find it relatively easy to narrow down your choices to one or two academic fields. If you can narrow it down to one, all the power to you.

The key here, of course, is that you've done a little (or a lot of) research. If you haven't looked around too much and the deadline for choosing a major approaches, you may have to make an uninformed decision. If you've looked around but don't know what to do with the information you've gathered, try writing it down on paper. Sometimes when we write things down they become much clearer in our minds, and that's the goal here. Write down some of the advantages and disadvantages of each field you're considering and include any particular features that stand out in your mind—how friendly the department head was when you approached her, how boring you found that 500-person intro class, and so on.

author's corner
▼
On the next page is a template that I used to help me make up my mind about a major. You don't have to use it, but it might help structure your thoughts.
▲

MAJOR	LEVEL OF INTEREST	QUALITY OF COURSES	PROFESSORS & ADVISORS
1. Sociology	High	Pretty good intro class; Interesting advanced courses	Intro prof was okay; Dept. head seems great
2.			
3.			
4.			
5.			

CONSIDER A DOUBLE MAJOR

If you're lucky enough to find not one passion but two—if you find yourself torn between two possible majors, both tugging at you with the same intensity and both filled with interesting and engaging classes—then perhaps it's time to think about a double major. Before you take this leap, though, there are a few important considerations that you need to keep in mind.

First of all, a double major can be very, very hard. You *will* be doing more work than your single-major classmates, and that extra work will start to take its toll after a couple of years. As your classes become more and more advanced, you'll find it harder to keep up with your coursework while maintaining a reasonable social and extracurricular life. And you'll have very few credits with which to explore other academic fields.

On the plus side, double majoring allows you to explore two potentially very different academic fields in reasonable depth. You'll truly be maximizing your college education if you can handle it. A double major leaves you more options for specializing in a certain field and pursuing graduate studies in it. It also looks quite impressive on a resume (but, of course, only if it's accompanied by a strong grade point average).

If you do choose to double major and later find that it wasn't a wise decision, you'll probably have the option to drop one of the fields in favor of the other. Find out what the deadlines and requirements for such decisions are, and keep them in mind. You should also talk to a few double majors about their experiences—try to find a few terrible experiences along with a few who give you wholehearted recommendations, so you can learn from both sides.

THINK ABOUT DESIGNING YOUR OWN MAJOR

"As far as I know, no one's ever done what I'm doing. That makes me feel just a little bit cooler."

Tibetan Mythology and Culture major, Rutgers '04

If you're feeling extremely adventurous, or if there doesn't seem to be anything in your school's course listings to match your freewheeling spirit, then you might just be a candidate for that rarest of all majors—the self-designed program. We must warn you, however: This option is *not* for the faint of heart. It requires a tremendous degree of focus, discipline, and commitment, and, perhaps most of all, the ability to drive and push yourself.

The first thing you should do is find out your school's particular approach to self-designed majors:

- Who will be your academic advisor—can you choose, or is one assigned to you?

- How many credits will you need in order to graduate?

- What about a thesis and honors—who will advise and evaluate your efforts?

Think about these sorts of questions now, before you commit yourself to anything specific.

You should also remember the potential advantages of being in a specific department. By choosing an established major, you become part of an academic community, one with a well-developed support system and a proven approach to study. There is much to be said for this sort of environment, and you should think long and hard before giving it up. Will you be able to find or create this type of a community with your self-designed major?

Above all, get a ton of advice—from students who've pursued their own majors, from professors who share your particular interests, and from advisors who can help you sort the practical issues. Make sure you know exactly what you're getting yourself into.

DON'T NEGLECT MINORS AND CONCENTRATIONS

Depending on your school, you might be able to choose a minor along with your major. Even if you don't have this option, you can select an unofficial minor by spending some of your electives on a field that interests you. Think of a minor as your secondary field of interest and focus—it will make up the second largest group of courses in your schedule, and you'll have the chance to explore it in considerable depth.

If you're interested in two academic fields but don't think that a double major is for you, then see if you can make one of them your minor. Find out if there are specific requirements for officially designating a minor and forge ahead.

Also give some thought to the concentration you can choose within your major. For example, history is a pretty broad field—perhaps you'll want to concentrate on a particular world region, time period, or even a particular event. You don't have to know what your concentration will be when you first choose your major, but it's something to consider as you begin your class selections.

MAKE UP YOUR MIND

"I had to choose a major halfway through sophomore year. It was pretty ugly, but I knew that it wasn't a lifelong commitment."

**Electrical Engineering major,
Cornell University '03**

At some point—probably around the middle of your sophomore year—you'll have to buckle down and choose a major (or two). No matter how much research you've done, this decision will probably feel a little scary. It's kind of like considering a marriage proposal—sure you're in love, but is he or she really the ONE?

By the time you have to commit yourself to a field, you'll hopefully have a reasonable idea of what you want to do. Take a last look through your notes, think for a bit, and make what you feel to be the best decision. It's not too terrible a moment—deep down, you probably know what the answer is. And whatever you choose, remember that it's not forever and that your college major will probably not define the rest of your life.

Take a deep breath. Follow your gut instincts. Trust your judgment.

author's corner
▾

I finally chose History and Literature as my major after looking over endless lists of requirements. I'm the kind of person who can't take fifteen classes on the same subject, so I looked for fields that offered a lot of variety and weren't very pushy about specializing. In the end, I settled for studying the entire canon of Western civilization and learning its complete history. It doesn't get much broader than that.

▲

changing your mind

"I felt like I was swimming in a current, being pushed in a certain direction day after day. I'm not sure what happened, but all of a sudden I was somewhere I didn't want to be."

**Zoology major,
University of Florida '03**

It happens all the time. You've been studying a field for a year, two years, and coasting happily along. Then it hits you: You hate what you're doing. It seemed great at first, but suddenly your classes are lethally boring, your bookshelves are lined with uninteresting books, and you can't remember the last time you had half an ounce of fun. With each passing day, you begin to wonder more and more whether you made a mistake.

First of all, relax. This sort of thing happens, and it will continue to happen as long as colleges and students coexist. The first question you should ask yourself is: Why am I so unhappy? Is it the field itself, the professors, the requirements? Is it the school?

If the problem seems to be with your chosen major—despite your best efforts to find a good one—then allow yourself to consider the possibility of switching to something different. It's okay to change your mind, even after a couple of years. Don't let yourself get stuck with something you don't enjoy—your time is way too valuable.

Here are a few steps to follow when you think you may want to change your major.

FIND THE PROBLEM
▼

FIX THE PROBLEM
▼

DEAL WITH PRACTICAL ISSUES

FIND THE PROBLEM

"After about a year of history, I realized that I couldn't take any more research paper assignments. I never seemed to be learning anything useful or interesting. I was digging up obscure facts about incidents that no one cares about. I finally had to ask myself, 'What's the point?' When I couldn't come up with an answer, I knew it was time to think about changing my major."

**Biological Sciences major,
Harvard University '03**

The first thing you should do is try to pinpoint the source of the problem. What is it that you dislike about your field? Is there something else you'd rather be doing? Questions like these can help you define your unhappiness in more useful terms. Don't immediately assume that the problem is with you, that you simply don't belong in college, and that you're incapable of liking academics. You probably just haven't found something that genuinely interests you. And in that you're definitely not alone.

One of the best ways to locate the source of trouble is to look over your grades for the last couple of years. In which classes did you do best and worst? A good grade is often an indication of extra effort on your part, and extra effort is often a sign of personal interest. Pay particular attention to poor grades in courses that you *had* to take because of your major but wouldn't have taken if it were your choice. These can often speak volumes about your interests and the conflicts you might be having with your field of study.

FIX THE PROBLEM

"I just couldn't get through my requirements because I hated chemistry so much. I thought I was going to die, and then I realized that I wouldn't have to take Organic Chemistry if I changed my major a little."

**Paleontology major,
University of Rhode Island '02**

Once you have a solid enough understanding of your central problem, you can look for ways to correct it. If you hate your field's requirements, look for a field with looser or more agreeable guidelines. If you can't stand the particular method by which your field is studied, look for a field that studies something in a different way. If you're simply bored with what you're studying, look for something more interesting (easier said than done, of course, but you *can* do it).

Choosing a major becomes progressively easier as you spend more time in college—you learn more about yourself and your interests with each passing day. By your second or third year, you've taken a few courses and (hopefully) considered a few fields. Bring this experience into the equation. What were some of your favorite classes? Was there ever an assignment that you *didn't* hate doing, and if so, what made this assignment more enjoyable than most? These kinds of questions, along with the kinds of inquiries you might have made when choosing your major in the first place (see "**getting acquainted with yourself**") will help you find a new line of study.

Changing your major can be a stressful and frustrating experience. But try to keep in mind that you're capable of getting through it and making your college experience more enjoyable in the process. You know exactly what you need to do—think about what bothers you and what interests you, talk to a few advisors and professors, and make a decision. Follow your instincts and, above all, TRUST YOURSELF. Ignore for a few moments the pressure you're probably feeling and let your own beliefs rule.

DEAL WITH PRACTICAL ISSUES

Once you've chosen a new field, you'll quickly have to deal with a few practical considerations. The most important, of course, is requirements. Do you have enough time to complete the required courses for your new major? If you're a junior or senior, you'll have fewer options: Many schools limit the number of terms you can attend and federal financial aid only covers eight semesters. Because some schools also have strict requirements for particular disciplines, your only choice might be a field similar to the one you're pursuing and one that has many similar requirements.

If you're not sure about requirements, take the time to talk to an advisor within the new department (see "**working with advisors**") and develop a plan of study. If all the practical issues are stacked against you, it may be impossible to change your field significantly. Even in this situation, you should still consider minor alterations to your track:

• Can you refocus on a different historical time period?

- Can you study French literature rather than French linguistics?

- Can you switch from microeconomics to macro?

You might find that making a change within your major will make you happier and more academically satisfied.

the daily grind

"I wish I'd been more organized about looking into departments. When the time came to make a decision, I didn't have any information I could use and I had to start from nothing. My roommate had his entire plan of study written out very neatly about two months into freshman year."

Economics major,
Georgia Tech '02

▶ MAKE TIME TO PLAN

Perhaps the biggest problem in researching fields is procrastination. You're so busy with classes and homework and friends that you can't seem to find the time to think about your future. The fact that you don't *want* to think about your future only makes it easier to put off. While there's no surefire way to conquer procrastination, you might want to consider scheduling a little time for research. If you write down, "READ ABOUT MAJORS" along with a time and date in your planner, scheduler, notebook, or whatever you often look at, you'll find it much harder to avoid doing the research.

Part of your research you're forced to do: You have to take classes, and there's no power in the universe that can spare you from this. Make time for the rest of your research—visiting professors, advisors, department heads, etc. If you put in a bit of effort now, you'll get a lot of payoff later.

►KEEP NOTES ON INTERESTING FIELDS

Everyone has his or her preferred note-taking apparatus. Some like the clipboard, some like notebooks, and some like tiny bits of paper in a pile. Whatever your method, make sure you write down the things you discover about each field. Don't trust your memory when it comes to this—you may come across ten to fifteen different fields in the four years you spend in college. Unless you have a photographic memory, you'll never be able to keep track of it all.

If your organizational skills leave much to be desired, use the simple template we put together (see "**settling down**").

► DON'T LET BAD ADVICE DERAIL YOUR AMBITIONS

> *"I got a letter from my mom every week, mostly telling me how glad she was I was going to be a doctor. I finally wrote back to her one day and said, 'Mom, would you want me operating on you?' She stopped mentioning medicine after that."*
>
> **English major,**
> **Yale University '03**

As you go through college, you'll hear many, many voices telling you what to do. There are good reasons for ignoring some of these voices, and good reasons for listening to others. You should always keep in mind that your judgments are primary—no one can tell you what you love or what you should do with your life (but they'll always try).

The advice you'll get in regard to choosing a major will generally fall into one of two categories: People telling you to think about your career and people telling you to follow your passion. Each of these categories has its merits, and it's up to you to strike the right balance between them. If you're lucky, you'll have a great four years followed by an exciting and satisfying career.

You'll probably get the most complicated and authoritative advice from your parents. They've been thinking about your college education and your career since the day you were born, and they'll certainly have an opinion as to where you should be headed. Try not to dismiss their advice outright, but don't allow yourself to follow their words blindly. The world is changing very quickly, and choices that made sense twenty years ago don't necessarily make any sense today. Talk to your parents, see if any of their advice helps you make decisions, but always try to stick to your own instincts.

what "they" say

We asked a few professors and advisors from Davidson, Harvard, Princeton, Stanford, and the University of Michigan to share their wisdom on major selection. Here's what they had to say.

WHAT WOULD YOU SAY TO A STUDENT TRYING TO CHOOSE A MAJOR?

"Look hard and long. Don't get stuck doing what you think you should be doing. College is expensive. Make the best of it."

"Shop, shop, shop, and don't get distracted by clearance sales and fancy banners. The best majors are usually the little ones, the ones with dusty old professors and magical books lurking in ancient bookshelves."

"Talk to everyone you know and write down their advice."

"Find a good advisor and stick to him or her. They'll help you immensely."

"Use the Internet whenever possible. You can get more research done online in a couple of hours than in a whole day of trekking. Every department will probably have a website, and every website will have at least some useful information. Read as much as you can, but make sure you pay a physical visit to the department if you have any unanswered questions."

TO WHAT EXTENT SHOULD STUDENTS CONSIDER THEIR CAREERS WHEN CHOOSING A MAJOR?

"*I don't think college is the place, at least initially, to decide the course of your life. College is the place to obtain a liberal arts education, to round yourself out as a human being.*"

"*You'll have time to think about that later. Your first couple of years, you shouldn't even know your favorite ice cream flavor, let alone the career you should pursue. Let your experiences guide your choices, and keep an eye out for the really cool jobs.*"

"*There are certain considerations you should keep in mind when choosing a major and one of them is undoubtedly your career. If you want to be a doctor or lawyer, you have to take steps early to meet requirements. Keep your options open, though. Look around as much as your track will allow and you might discover something unexpected.*"

"*You should do what you LOVE. Getting a job is easy. Getting a job you like requires that you have some experience in listening to yourself.*"

WHEN SHOULD A STUDENT DECIDE ON A MAJOR?

"I'd say around the end of sophomore year. Even if your school makes you do it earlier, you can just fudge that and choose your real major later."

"The decision should take place in several steps. Narrow your choices from four or five to two or three and down to one. You should probably make it to the end of that ladder by the last couple of months of your sophomore year. There might be time to step back later, but you have to make a commitment."

"Whenever you find something you really love. It might take a month, it might take four years. If you need to spend eight years in college to find something you like, then that's how long you should be there. If that's not possible at your school, go someplace else."

helpful resources

We spent a bit of time looking for some helpful books and we found a few that you might find useful. Remember that your own college or university probably has many great resources—booklets, websites, etc.—to help you think through your options. Take advantage of them. You have to make your own decisions, but that doesn't mean you have to make them in isolation.

Major in Success: Make College Easier, Fire up Your Dreams, and Get a Very Cool Job, by Patrick Combs, Jack Canfield. Ten Speed Press, 3rd Edition, April 2000.

A high-energy book to help you discover your interests, passions, career, and life goals. It's written by a not-so-long-ago grad, and we think you'll appreciate the peer perspective.

What Every College Student Should Know: How to Find the Best Teachers and Learn the Most from Them, by Ernie Lepore and Sarah-Jane Leslie. Rutgers University Press, March 2002.

This concise and efficient little book will help you with seeking out the best professors and the most interesting classes, which will give you a slight edge in your major-hunting process.

The College Majors Handbook: The Actual Jobs, Earnings, and Trends for Graduates of 60 College Majors, by Paul E. Harrington, Thomas F. Harrington, Neeta P. Fogg. Jist Works, January 1999.

While we've harped on the fact that your major doesn't have to be connected to a particular career, you might find it helpful to learn about your options. There aren't enough truly useful books on this subject, but this one can give you a pretty good overview of what students with certain majors have gone on to do in their lives.

McGraw Hill publishes a whole series of books with career ideas for various majors. They're titled "Great Jobs for English Majors," "Great Jobs for Psychology Majors," and so on. You might find them useful as you ponder your major selection. Nearly all are available online, and they won't set you back more than eleven or twelve dollars.

the final word

We're all afraid of making mistakes—life sometimes seems to be an endless series of opportunities to mess up. The best bit of advice we can give you in the last moments of this guide is this: DON'T BE AFRAID. Life is short, college is shorter, and your only responsibility is to get the most out of what you're given. Choosing the right major is one giant step in that direction.

Doctors say that the best way to keep your mind strong and alert is to do something new every day. As the four years of college fly past you (and, oh, how the years DO fly), make sure to hold on to your sense of adventure. Never let yourself fall into doing the expected or the ordinary. Instead, take a chance, venture into unfamiliar fields, and surprise yourself. If you don't like what you're learning, change it. What do you have to lose?

However scary this might sound, you're in control of your own destiny. Make it one that makes you happy.

4527

To learn more about **Students Helping Students™**
guides, read samples, share your own experiences with
other students, suggest a topic or ask questions, visit us at
www.studentshelpingstudents.com!